DEEP FROM MY HEART

Edited by

Rebecca Mee

First published in Great Britain in 2001 by
POETRY NOW
Remus House,
Coltsfoot Drive,
Peterborough, PE2 9JX
Telephone (01733) 898101
Fax (01733) 313524

HB ISBN 0 75432 527 X
SB ISBN 0 75432 528 8

FOREWORD

Although we are a nation of poets we are accused of not reading poetry, or buying poetry books. After many years of listening to the incessant gripes of poetry publishers, I can only assume that the books they publish, in general, are books that most people do not want to read.

Poetry should not be obscure, introverted, and as cryptic as a crossword puzzle: it is the poet's duty to reach out and embrace the world.

The world owes the poet nothing and we should not be expected to dig and delve into a rambling discourse searching for some inner meaning.

The reason we write poetry (and almost all of us do) is because we want to communicate: an ideal; an idea; or a specific feeling. Poetry is as essential in communication, as a letter; a radio; a telephone, and the main criterion for selecting the poems in this anthology is very simple: they communicate.

CONTENTS

LOVED TO DEATH

I loved him to death,
focused my life around him,
filled entire days thinking of him.

Twenty years on
like new lovers
we never had our fill.

I could not imagine
life without him.
He was my life - blood, body and soul.

Yet, still it happened.
He couldn't bear to be
the one left behind.

I couldn't either.
But: I loved him to death
couldn't watch . . .

watch him suffer,
lose his uniqueness
with the slow trickle of time.

It wasn't easy
sending him on his way.
I loved him to death

as in life, he . . .
my centre
. . . and beyond.

Sue Hansard

BECAUSE

Because again you've sneaked away
and left me,
ringless,
I vow I'll see you no more.
No more shared beds
in rented rooms.
No more waking at dawn
to find you gone,
leaving a depression in my pillow
to match the one you've left
in my head.

Doreen Dean

DROWNED HER

She swam in on the early tide
rotten to the core
a raft for gulls
naked and ashamed
she wrapped herself in seaweed
lay in a huddle
in a pool beyond the shoreline.

She moves slowly
through still waters
wrapped up in leaves
all her fingers reach to me
and I swoop down
to run my fingers
through her hair.
She smiles in ripples
and if it weren't for the drowning
we'd hold hands.

James Noonan

HANGING ON THE AIR . . .

She sits there, restless eyes, fingers twirling strand of hair,
Trying to hide her pain, but it hangs on the air
Between us.
Tenacious yet elusive, its face evades us,
Neither of us prepared to reach out and catch it,
Or look at it, or touch it;
Afraid perhaps of its sting,
Its backlash, its ugliness.
And I sit there with restless love -
Longing to slip past her pain
And hug her.
But they come as a pair, the two of them together;
And I cannot bear to touch pain's roughness again so soon.
Too fragile, me, for now.

Suffering in silence thus, the two of us sit -
Empathy and anguish hanging on the air -
Each waiting for the other to make a move.
And her pain knows me too well.
It will have me sooner or later.
And she sits there reaching out,
Restless eyes, fingers twirling strand of hair -
Waiting.

Jenny Proom

SOUL MATE

Some fleeting thought, unuttered yet,
A breath within the mind
Some secret pulse for me alone,
And not for her to find

And yet I sense intrusion there,
Some subtle, tender snare
To rob me of my hiding place,
My covert thoughts laid bare

But not for her alone to probe,
The muted ebbs and flows
Silent traces, ill disguised,
Are there for me to know

Windows of the soul they say,
Deep hazel pools invite
Heralds of a promise pledged,
Unspoken thoughts excite

Silken threads caress my cheek,
Sweet scented musk incites
Intertwining fingers speak,
Encoded words unite

Closer now, the fragrant lure,
The breath within the mind
Is breath no more, but living force
And free for her to find.

Stan Herbert

INCENTIVE

The earth is often shadowed,
death hovers overhead
like angels ready to transport
my soul to peace,
yet one flame leaps with loving,
with joy, with constant pride;
she sings, my child, and all is nought
but sweet release.
Out of tumult glows her face,
her captivating grin
eradicating eager hells,
giving me heart.
Eyes speak from confining walls,
reflective as mirrors.
I know shame and vision propels
me to start
reaping the harvest of dreams,
of breathing for her,
she who beseeches me survive.
I love her so;
my girl, honied with music,
caressing guitar;
she laughs, and I must stay alive,
that much I know.

Ruth Daviat

DEEP IN THE WEST-WOOD'S WOMB

This is the place where my innocence died,
And this is the site of her tomb -
Here, where the brushwood and sheaf may hide,
Deep in the West-Wood's womb.

Here, where the needles lie smooth and soft,
And the hush of the pinewood reigns,
Where night, though the summer be bright aloft,
'Neath the lowest boughs remains.

This is the path where my innocence walked -
Her slayer and she hand in hand.
An unknowing infant, she laughed and talked,
And her feet fell light on the sand.

He led her in here, full of infinite trust.
Here life's frail and silky strands
Were found and severed with the tender touch
Of pale inexperienced hands.

Here, where the twilight is one with the trees,
Where no stardust sifts through from above,
My innocence sleeps with a childlike ease,
Secretly murdered by love.

Nina Havers

ULSTER'S MILLENNIUM PRAYER

The rainbows end elusive,
A commodity most rare,
And likewise peace in Ulster,
And few that seem to care.
Politicians line their pockets,
MLA to millionaire,
How many of them can we trust?
How many of them care?

This search for peace continues,
But strife deep-rooted lies,
We cling to our traditions,
We must not compromise.
The struggle will continue
Viewpoints remain entrenched,
The hand of friendship idle,
The trigger hand still clenched.

'Twas peace on earth the angels sang,
The truth is plain to see,
For God alone can bring us peace,
His Son our peace must be.
This peace is based on sacrifice,
Great love - a wondrous gift,
This peace from Calvary floweth,
To mend the deepest rift.

We want no fickle, fragile peace,
No peace with threat impending,
We want a peace eternal,
A peace that's never ending.
Man's heart must be the vital source,
A heart from God above,
Self seeking decommissioned,
A heart that's filled with love.

God grant such peace in Ulster,
God knows that's what we need,
Not based on priest or prelate,
Not based on cult or creed.
So in God's hands we leave our woes,
God's people trust and pray,
That very soon a land of peace,
Godspeed that glorious day.

Stephen Shanks

MADRUGADA VIAJE

Is that all he wants after sipping wine
Red as lust - to be on the moon
When he could have Andromeda, sublime
Spiral faint of eyelids, in his arms?

Is that all she wants when the wine is gone
Pale as the night - to be on the land.
Not hand on heart with Orion
Tripping through hot starry showers, sword in hand.

Lips tremble against the coolness of glass;
Cool glass from shifting molten sand.
Quenching liquid heady feeling, a mist,
Soft drop object to the floor: Land.

Moves off, rapturous glance in each tipsy eye.
Fingertips reach out for satellites
But vista remains majestic Spanish sky
After small hours in return of daylight.

Suzanne Stratful

LOVE HEART TO HEART

Love is good each day at a time
If you fight love it will bring you together
Love gets stronger every day and every year,
When you go through pain and every emotion.
Love is always there for some people and
Everybody it can last forever and forever.
Love is hot and lust, yum, yum, when you're in love
You're hot and excited, they can be your best friend.
Love is hot and sexy, when you're sad you need your love.
To be there for you when you go through bad times,
Sometimes close to your heart but you need your loved one
To be there and feel wanted and needed.
Love is a shoulder to cry on, love gets hard though
Not easier, love is special.
Heart to heart words can't speak more than
Love, I never hurt anyone, I love everyone,
Never blaming people close to you special.
The loved one's heart to heart,
Love is special and love is blind.
Love is all around the world,
Everyone can find love,
Love is heart to heart,
Close to your love and heart
Love is all around the world,
That way love is heart to heart.

Tina Jones

A TURNING POINT

Sombre thoughts pervade my head,
One vision had me lying dead,
Pale and still upon my bed,
Swept me into a watershed.

Waking up to a life surmountable,
Realising that I am accountable,
Knowing that this world's redoubtable,
I now find sombre thoughts contemptible.

Hugh S McKay

WHY AM I SO SAD?

Why am I so really sad?
Why do I feel this bad?
My heart has sunk so deep,
Making me cry in my sleep,
Smiling is such a chore,
Tears from my eyes, pour,
Another's love I do miss,
No more sweet lips to kiss,
Hands no longer in mine,
All my joy out of time,
Inside, my being is dead,
Much hurt within my head,
Am I the only sad one?
Now my true love has gone.

Christopher Higgins

ETERNAL LOVE

A friend,
Is someone who shares;
Who feels your pain,
Who is always there to comfort.

A friend,
Is someone who cares;
Who celebrates your joy,
Who wishes you well.

A friend,
Believes in you,
Finds you special;
In you, frees all.

A friend,
Is someone who is a rock.

The song,
What a friend I have in Jesus;
Embracing the beauty,
Of dependable constancy.

Eternal love,
Within the bosom,
Of Christ;
For all believing.

To have as your pillar,
For all time,
Humility - strength - wisdom - care;
Is to have, a unique friend.

Rowland Warambwa

How Do I Love Thee

How do I love thee child of mine
So much, I cried tears of joy you were so divine
I gazed at you and could not believe
You were there for me and no reprieve.

Time progressed and changes took place
Each one an experience I would not replace
There were days when you were a naughty child
So much, my temper was really not mild!

But as the span of life sped by
You became so much a part of me
You were my friend, my advisor, my joy
And you kept me young.

Now comes the time when I have to be strong
A young man has fallen in love with you
I wasn't surprised, for your lovely smile
Made me fear I should lose you in a while.

I knew he had become your special Beau
A mother feels these things you know,
I am happy for you dear so when you depart
Remember you will also be taking a piece of my heart.

Hazel Devonshire

WHAT IS LOVE?

What is this thing called love?
What is it that makes my heart race
whenever I hear my beloved's voice?
That power in a smile that lifts my soul
that burns through flesh and bone to reach the heart!
That certain look in sapphire eyes
That melts my heart to jelly!

Is this the passion of love?
Is it true what I see in my beloved's beautiful face
our lives entwined into one heavenly joy!
For long ago beloved you planted love in my heart
and like the fragrant rose it has grown there
blossomed forth strong true and loyal
'oh yes' love hurts for like the rose love has its thorns
but also like the rose loves perfume is beyond compare!

Love speaks to your heart, lightens your soul!
the passion of love is like a fire glowing in the heart
for I would lay my life bare and bleed myself dry
for the love of my beloved
my beloved is more precious that gold or silver to me
my beloved is my sun by day and moon by night
and in the shade of my beloved I will rest my weary soul
until my life on this mortal earth is ended?

James Ellis

My Darling David

I will always love you David, I promise I always will
and when this world stops turning, I'll be loving you still.
Until hell freezes over and clouds fall from the skies,
you'll know my powerful love, when you look into my eyes.

I'll wear your ring with dignity, I'll wear your ring with pride,
my promise to you I'll keep, from the day I become your bride.
To honour and cherish, to love and obey,
to say 'I do,' to you, won't be hard for me to say.

I'll love this way forever and I know that we can make it,
my every breath of life, I'm giving you to take it.
I know we'll have our problems, but together we'll see them through,
cos, now from this day forward, there'll be no one for me, but you.

Mary Hoey

MY FATHER

He held me in his gentle arms
When I was just a child,
I looked into his hardened face
He kissed me then he smiled.

He taught me how to say my name
Then how to read and write,
He taught me everything he knew
To me he was always right.

He guided me through all the years
His words were always good,
He was always there when I needed him
He'd help me all he could.

Now he's gone and I'm alone
But his memory lives right on,
For a man I loved so dearly
My father will never be gone.

Myrddin Jones

What Then Is Love?

We cannot measure love
For it has no weight,
Nor height, nor depth,
For like the wind
It cannot be seen,
Yet we experience love.
Without love we are nothing
Nor can love be bought
Love cannot be sold,
We can give love
We receive love.
What then is love
Which lasts for ever,
Is it a conundrum of life?
Maybe in a word
Love *is*.

David A Garside

GRANNY'S LOVE FOR HOLLY

Snowflakes are falling
We're three hundred miles apart,
I think of your wee happy, smiling face
And you warm up my heart.

My darling little Holly,
With your sparkling eyes of sapphire blue,
I can hardly believe it
That you will soon be two.

You've brought so much love and joy
Into my life,
Since the day that you were born
You are a little angel
Captured in your tiny form.

Love, it knows no boundaries,
It reaches out o'er all the miles
I would travel hundreds
For just one of your smiles.

Kathleen Morrison

TRUE INNOCENCE

Children's joy in picking flowers
Glowing faces of honest delight
Noses buried deep in blossoms
Gentle innocence, in full sight.

What a photo, for the camera
Posing, unrequired there
Natural movement, natural beauty
A permanent picture, for all to share.

Bouquets collected for their mothers
Given with a genuine love
Who cannot, but be emotional
When a child presents a 'dove.'

Naughty children are forgiven
Overwhelming love to share
Children soon turn into adults
Time will pass, there's none to spare.

Be grateful for God's gift of children
And love they give, without thought
They must be cherished, without exception
Love like theirs, can not be bought.

Idwal B Holt

LOVING DAYS

I loved you so when only four
Playing on a rocky shore.
Loved you still when nearly seven -
Picking brambles - sheerest heaven.
Came the teens, dropped a book
Paddling in a minnowed brook
Loving you, a youthful fool
Dawdling crazily home from school
Prayed to die at college start.
You went away and took my heart.
Just to see your eyes of grey
Set me back for many a day.
To see you capped and neatly gowned -
Hastily, I look around.
Loved filled eyes meet and smother
How I do love you. My Big Brother.

Marnie Connley

On The Death Of My Husband

Damp, sweaty sheets, feverish brow,
Eyes stabbed by the light -
We'll use candlelight now.

I hold your hand gently,
I keep my voice low,
There's so much to say, love,
Before you let go.

We have much to remember,
Down the years we have shared -
Children and laughter
And joy uncompared.

There's been sadness and sorrow
But our love has been true -
We've faced problems together
And always won through,

And now, you are drifting,
You've nothing to fear,
Your pain will soon vanish -
Angel wings hover near,

In the midst of this anguish,
I ask you, 'Lord, why?'

But ask not who is dying, love,
I know that it is I.

Jane Finlayson

TRUE LOVE NEVER DIES

I returned once more to the house beside the Thames,
A place rich in achievement and cultural history
Where the ghosts of William Morris, Burne-Jones and Rossetti
Are as palpable as the river which flows past in perpetuity.

I remembered the first time you took me
Through a small door in the old wall,
And how we walked across the wide expanse of grass
With you beside me, upright, mature and tall.

Your flat revealed traces of a wandering life
As an exile and man of many parts;
We looked at the faded albums of your travels
And talked of poetry, music and the arts.

We sat as the shadows crept towards the house
Casting elongated fingers in the room,
Our features becoming softly obscured
Against the advancing gloom.

In a silence more eloquent than words
We remained, not quite touching, face to face,
And then, with the unspoken thought between us
We were spinning and merging in an endless embrace.

There were long afternoons of shared passion,
Its exquisite flame suffusing every minute, hour and day
So that the world and the distant roar of traffic
Could have been a million miles away.

You bestowed on me the wealth of your experience
As teacher, lover and now my unseen friend.
I realised as I stood alone by the river
That true love cannot die and must prevail in the end.

Rosina Winiarski

OH FRAGILE HEART

Spears of sunlight pierce the mist
The end is nigh for the lovers' tryst
Wrapped in each other like ivy round a tree
With the dawn they know their love cannot be.

Cobwebs hanging from the pine
Decked with tears of dew they shine
Like mine the tears on my lover's face
Locked arm in arm, one last embrace.

Why does the world interfere with this plight?
The love of my life will be gone by tonight
Strength eludes us to stand our ground
For such love which had grown sound.

Oh fragile heart why feel such pain
Will my lover wend one's way back to me again?
Until then I'll shut the door
I'm shattered, a million pieces fall on the floor.

Jean Parker

LOVE

Dimmed skies
Swelled with rain
My heart is full

Mad with love
The bird swoons

Silent fear
With baited breath
Wounds the mind

Love is a madness
It twists and tortures
Tormented so
In pools of silver
The shining bird
Lies silent.

Rosey Moffatt

THE STAR BY WHICH I SAIL MY SHIP

You are the star by which I sail my ship
The destination marked upon my chart,
On my echo radar you are the blip
As I navigate the seas of your heart.

For you I would cross the deepest oceans
Suffer squalls and tempests and storm force gales.
In this leaky boat I call my emotions
This armada of feelings that I sail.

I pray fair winds will not abandon me
And keep this sailor on course and high tide,
On this voyage I single handedly
Aim to drop anchor by your harbour side.

Where this old sea dog before it's too late,
Will try to press gang you to be first mate.

Keith Tissington

THE BONDING

The demands of loving
The nestling in, the seeking for comfort,
For the life-giving streams of nourishment
Flowing between us.
The gentle touch of tiny hands
Brushing over me like butterfly wings
Claiming infant ownership.
Wide awake blue eyes, searching, finding
Focus on my face
Engaging my rapt concentration
Mutual harmony
Reflecting the hidden impulses
Which pass between us.
Dropping, replete
Heavy with sleep,
Tiny head cradled
Against my warm body,
Sleep, sleep, secure
In love's warmth.

Beryl Johnson

FOREVER YOURS

You took me and shaped me
I belong entirely to you.
My body, heart, mind and soul
Are yours now and always.
You are my love, my life and all
That matters to me.
Without you I would rather die
Than live.
I owe you so much, thank you
For always being there for me, for
Putting me right when I was wrong.
I am what you have made me,
Forever yours.

Sue Cox

REAL LOVE

What is real love?
No one can really say,
We each are different
In many a way,
I saw you and fell in love
Had eyes for only you,
You asked for my hand
Couldn't wait to say, 'I do,'
Each day was so exciting
My heart missed a beat,
Every time I saw your face
You swept me off my feet.

Now we have reached the twilight years
But still our love is there,
Reminisce on days gone by
So much love we share,
It may seem to others
That we are very old,
They cannot see what's in our hearts
The cherished love we hold,
We do not see our wrinkle face
Don't worry very much,
As long as we have each other
We know that loving touch.

J Naylor

LOVE OF LIFE

Love can be a very open book
And you can say mountains with just one look.
You are sure the coming hours will be full of treasure,
So you view all around with much pleasure.

The day is fresh and so are you,
So try to bring happiness in all that you do.
Your path will be far smoother you will find,
When golden memories are the first to spring to mind.

Others will thank you for helping them to see,
How joy is able to set one free.
Your joy springs from the heart
And you'll find it so much easier to
Play a useful part.

Betty Green

ONE DAY, MY TRUTH WILL BE KNOWN

Silently, whispers in the night.
Dreaming, of a world where we can be free.
Hopeful, that you might be there with me.
Knowing, that your love for me understands.

I am not the perfect one,
I have so many failings,
but, like so many who have lived
I am not the best,
and I am not the worst.
So, I am Miss Average,
and what is so very wrong with that?

I cannot tell you everything
that lies within my hidden heart,
but I cannot hide away forever.
A time will come when I will know
no fear or apprehension.
I will talk clearly and you will know
what I know without hate.

You, who have told me so much
about the life that is you,
will no longer feel that you are
without a soul to share with,
without a heart to call home.
I do not want to be hidden,
or keep myself secret from you.

Silently, whispers in the night.
Dreaming, of a world where we can be free.
Hopeful, that you might be there with me.
Knowing, that your love for me understands.

Angela G Pearson

A FIGHT FOR LOVE

I remember the joy that once filled my heart
The night we first met and destiny played its part.
Out of the darkness that enveloped my soul
You held my hand tightly, made me feel whole!

Oh how we laughed, like we never had before
Reached out to each other, searching no more
Happiness engulfed us, infusing the air
Enchanting, translucent, people stopped to stare!

A love like ours was a gift from above
I worshipped the ground you walked on, showered you with love
We planned our future together, come what may,
Left the past behind us, thought we'd found the right way!

But the storm clouds were coming, why didn't I see
That my idyllic contentment was no longer to be?
Who was this stranger with hate in his eyes,
Throbbing vein on temple, my love in disguise?

I cowered and shrank from this monster unknown
Fear and pain clutched my heart leaving me lost and alone
Confusion descended, I knew this wasn't right
Then the abrupt awakening - another love I must fight!

I tried to beguile you, to steer you away
Flaunted my charms, silently begging you to stay.
But the battle was too big to fight on my own
We both needed help now the enemy was known!

Together hand in hand we bravely explored,
After me pleading and crying that help should be sought,
So our bond was then strengthened, our love ever true
But waiting in the background, my rival beckoned you.
And as you raised your glass - gulped it down in one
My battle for love over, the drink had finally won!

Carol Ann Jones

I'LL BE THERE
(Dedicated to my darling Joyce)

If you ever need me I'll be there
I will bring you comfort when you are sad
I will show you that I care, and
Share your grief when times are bad.

I'll be there with you in the dead of night
When you can't sleep to get your rest
To keep you safe till morning light, and
Gently soothe your savage breast.

I'll bring you love to fill your heart
With happiness to fill your every day
I'll hold you in my thoughts while we're apart
I'll be there beside you when you pray.

I'll be there for you forever
Hold you in love's golden band
My love is such that nought can sever
I'll hold you in my powerful hand.

Keep the love and faith I give
Take it in good measure
Take it, then in your heart I'll live
Close to you forever.

J W Hewing

LOVE SUPREME

'Who am I?' You ask me, 'What use on earth am I?'
For years you've struggled on your own.
With no one to love you, not knowing why.
You met me and I met you, trust blossomed deeply between us two.
Love followed quickly, though neither of us knows why.
Love and trust help us to fly so high.
I can't answer for the others, or say why they couldn't see,
the 'You' that God revealed to me, or the 'Me' that He revealed to you.
But there in lies God's will for us, a love to last till the end of time.
Sometimes it seems easier not to love, it seems to cause
                                            less personal pain.
Yet that's not true, getting involved is worth it, for our love
                                            supreme to reign.
God loves us deeply, we both know it's true.
We know the world is fickle, that other loves have changed.
That greed, anger and self pity, have other lives rearranged.
But I am me and you are you, we don't have to be like
                                            others me and you.
For in each other's eyes we are special, with a love that is so rare.
What matters most for both of us, is that of each other's love
                                            we are aware.
The sun would shine less brightly, the sky would be less blue.
If we were not together under God's heaven - me and you.
I'll show every day of my life, how happy and proud I
                                            am to be your wife.
So please don't question the reason why - because my love
                                            for you will never die.

Margi Hughes

LOST YOUTH

There could have been another one,
But my first love was the best.
Somehow he seemed just set apart
And different from the rest.

Though I could have been contented
With a third love, even four.
They didn't measure up to him,
For he had something more.

I waited, more than four long years,
The war kept us apart
And shed a thousand, thousand tears,
For he took with him my heart.

And though he came home safely
No country could repay -
The loss of happy, carefree youth
Those war years took away!

Molly Rodgers

CONNECTION

This is when you
Know it is right
When our days
Seems like nights.

Walk quickly with me
Very very briskly
Where will the dust be
Without the wind to blow it free?

How will the rain fall
If there is no gravity
How will the clouds float high?
If its compounds were not light.

Let's take time with our lives
Follow the flow of the rivers
And just float
Let's go.

It is a lonely place
When it is dark
When there are no
Sun or stars.

Like me
I am also lonely
When you are not close
To my heart.

Nathaniel L A Gabriel-Lovell

THE EQUILIBRIUM OF FRIENDSHIP

Friendship is like the smell of scrambled eggs on toast.
Friendship is like the things you desire most.
Friendship is like warming toes, when you are cold.
Friendship is like, the sight of a baby, one minute old.
Friendship is like a special tenderness.
Friendship is like an annual bonus, no less.
Friendship is like the aroma of freshly baked bread.
Friendship is like the beauty of sunsets of red.
Friendship is like a stretched out hand when you fall.
Friendship is like the strength of a solid brick wall.
Friendship is like a breath of clean fresh air.
So try to offer friendship to all everywhere.

To my friends, I wish everything that is the best.
To my enemies, I just wish to say 'God bless.'

Yvonne Chapman

A SPECIAL LOVE

My life was empty, so alone
A wandering soul without a home
But all that changed when I met you
You really were that 'dream come true'

It's not the special things we do
(All time is special when with you)
It's the times we talk, and laugh, and cry
How we loathe to say goodbye.

The things you do, the words you say
Make me feel special every day
I know you love, I know you care
I know that you are always there.

It isn't just on Valentine's Day
That I'll tell you how I feel
I intend to tell you every day
Of every single year.

For you have given life to me
And love I never knew
And I hope for many years to come
I shall share my all with you.

Heather Thomas

THE GIFT

His love for me is dead and cold,
My soul's in disrepair.
My heart is ripped to ribboned shreds,
A rabbit in a snare.

He's bequeathed to me his azure eyes,
His hair of amber gold.
He's given me his fetching glance,
His warm smile to behold.

Then why am I so worn and torn,
Bruised, broken and beguiled?
It's because this token so bestowed
Is invested in our child.

The years move on, sore wounds have gone,
My Son has now matured;
He's a gift to me, a legacy,
Worth all the pain endured.

Susan Jarvis

RED ROSES

Red roses I send -
to interpret my devotions.
Only through these roses
can I explain my emotions,
too shy and withdrawn I know I
Often appear,
Yet! Sending you roses I know draws
us near.

The thoughts I constant endure,
and the love I now impart,
are shared through a rose.
I know not any other way to start,
to say I do love you, my darling dear.
I thank the Lord for keeping you near.

Red roses now foretell my inner desires,
my hopes that marriage surely transpires,
if both our wishes -
emerge at last as one,
I know my victory shall be won

accept the red roses that I give,
which say - without you I
could not live.
Then shall I know deep in my heart,
I chose the right girl from the start.

Steve Kettlewell

LOVE IN DEPTH

Love to me
Means many many things
From the beautiful places
To the birds that sing.

To see breathtaking scenery
As you pass by
To see birth of new life
Brings a tear to your eye.

But most of all
I'll have to say
Is to have the warmth of your family
Close by every day.

My wife is so special
To me she's the one
Without her love
True sadness would come.

My daughter means so much
So proud I am of her
I'll give her love for the future
So great things will occur.

Also not forgetting
My brothers, family and friends
Help and good intentions
Always to send.

But without love from my mum
And without love from my dad
These great things couldn't happen
And I would be sad.

Rob Passmore

WHERE

Tell me where that place is
where there are faces
I used to know;
Where there are quiet spaces
in Time's fast flow
when the hands of the clock are slow
and each day encases
close ones closeness which has the glow
of substance and not mere traces
in the haze of an old tomorrow.
There I know now that grace is
and those I gladly hallow.
Tell me where that place is
and I will go.

Ken Merry

YOU'RE WONDERFUL

Tall, dark and handsome, so they say
Nearing thirty, next May
An abundance of designer labels
Randy and at play with a workout
Every other day
Then I met you.

My feelings for you have permeated
Every corner of my being.
I feel sick.
I ponder, I visualise, I scheme
For time with you, I dream.

Today, the sky is a brighter blue
Then I have ever seen
My sense of smell has heightened
I'm filled with anticipation like a
                child at Hallowe'en.

Yet, two weeks ago I knew not of you
I worked competitively with distractions few
My mobile and e-mails were the centre of my earth
I felt grounded, each deal my rebirth.

Has something happened to my mind
How can two strangers be so quickly mentally entwined?
Perhaps it's true, love can come like a bolt from the blue
Forsaking logic and reason too.

Gloria Hargreaves

Taken Young

Mother dear - it still stays hard to fill the passing years
From the day you left us when so young, not to feel your
tender loving hands of care. Knowing your honest thoughts,
were always for our good, the value of your tender loving
ways will never leave me, in my fading years and still to
this day I can be as one with you, mother, you are always
dear to me.

Rowland Patrick Scannell

You Are The Catalyst

You are the Catalyst, that lights my fire,
You're my one true burning desire,
You spark the flame that burns within,
You set my heart ablaze again.

You wrote the song I long to sing,
You sang it back to me again,
What more can I do?
You know, I'd give my love to you.

Your lips are warm and tender,
They bid my heart to surrender,
As into your arms I did fall,
Now by your side I feel so tall.

Content to lie there by your side,
And rest awhile on your bed wide,
Awaiting morning's light to shine,
Now I know that you are mine.

Your love, it still ignites my soul,
And fills my life with desire untold,
You set my very heart aflame,
With passion true, and love so new.

And when we kiss and touch afresh,
That's the time we both love best,
You are the Catalyst, that lights my fire,
You are still, my true desire.

David Watkins

ALL MY CHILDREN

I never had a girl or boy,
I'd never met a lad
With whom I might have known such joy
As lucky parents had.

Nor later, did I find a man,
Of those who courted me
I'd trust to change my lifetime's plan
Or Father's equal be.

Yet little ones I gladly served
And gave them of my best,
Toddlers to teens their ways observed,
When happy, when distressed.

At not quite two small David said
A sentence, 'Open door!'
A prophesy for years ahead
As they new worlds explore?

And joy it was when eager minds
My teaching gave me back,
As any loving parent knows
Who tries to show life's track.

The boys and girls who talked with me,
From whom I learnt each day,
Themselves may now grandparents be
And half a world away.

Not Solomon's wives and porcupines
(As so the schoolboy said)
Could ever start so many lines
As these, my children, spread.

It's good to know, when age has come,
That once one was a surrogate mum!

Kathleen M Hatton

WINTER OF LOVE

Had walked a lonely day or two
Through heartache and rain,
Lived an English winter
Of loneliness and then,
Love surfaced from the forest floor,
From the undergrowth of pain,
The leaves were brushed from pathways
And the sun shone bright again.
Once stagnant ponds were brought to life
As nature took its course,
Love fed the saplings and the heart
Was cleared from forest moss.
The flowers bloomed, the heathers grew,
The grass returned to green.
The Kingdom once so overgrown,
Now reigned again, supreme.

Alan Glendinning

SATIN LACE

As I close my eyes
I see your smiling face
As I close my eyes
You're there, in satin lace.

Is it a dream, or my imagination?
Is it love, or a hallucination?
I must have you for my own
So do not leave me all alone.

As I close my eyes
I see your smiling face
As I close my eyes
You're there, in satin lace.

Down the aisle, hand in hand
To a future so grand
God's blessing, and happiness
Will bring us joy and success.

As I close my eyes
I see your smiling face
As I close my eyes
I am in your embrace.

William A Laws

THAT CERTAIN FEELING
FOR DORRIE

My love has auburn hair intertwined with
Golden flames, rich and warm and bronze and soft
To touch and finely scented.
My love's anatomy is fiery curved
With hallowed heartbeat wondrously embalmed
In powerfully feline grace from shoulder
Through curvature of waist to moulded thigh,
Divine to gaze upon.
My love's own eyes are marvellous keen in sheen.
Their magic spell they cast in laughing gaze.
Access to the Maker does she give and
I am humble in her praise.
My love is perfect in her temperament -
Calm, serene, agelessly wise in her
Contentment, innocently knowing.

May she be mine for ever.

Desmond Tarrant

ETERNAL FLAME

My love for you will never die,
it sparkles like a diamond in the sky.
It glows like the embers of a fire in the night,
burning hot and bright.

Once I set you free,
then the embers died.
Only for the flames to return again
when you breezed back into my life.

Now the flame of our love,
burns true, white and bright.
Eternally,
lighting up our nights.

Stewart Lyell

DEAR FRIEND

I remember the years
When life was so gay,
I remember companionships
Which we shared each day,
But nothing can ever reconcile,
The way I remember,
Your wonderful smile.

I remember your courage
No matter the strife,
I remember your kindness
Which took you through life,
Your thoughts were of others
To make life worthwhile
But how well I remember
Your wonderful smile.

Margaret Brunton

ANDY'S EYES

When I close my eyes I still can see
The way your eyes smiled back at me.

Young, playful eyes, filled with fun
As you sat there, with Phyllis and John.

I never believed in love at first sight,
But I fell for you on that fateful night.

I knew, before I'd got back on the bus
That I'd really and truly fell in love.

Oh, and God, it was lovely to feel
So truly uplifted - it was so unreal.

You've heard of the saying 'If looks could kill.'
Well I could have died for those eyes
And I probably still will.

Tell me Andy - why did it go so wrong
When I felt so much for you all along?

All I now seem to get is a sniggering glare
But I'm doubting whether you ever cared.

But even when you're selfish and rude
I still know what those eyes can do.

And when I close my eyes I still can see
Your gorgeous eyes smiling back at me.

Josephine Reading

LOVE IS

Love is a flower
Learns about nature,
Blossoms and grows
Love is us together
Love is when you know.

Love is used by many
But mustn't be misused
Love should last forever
Two people make it grow.

Love is fun
Caring, understanding
Love is tender
Incredibly demanding.

Love is a word
Which explains how you feel
Love is certainly something
It's incredibly real.

Tracy Charters

BODY LANGUAGE

It's in the eyes, it's in the vibes,
The way you stare, there are no lies,
To stand quite near, to feel the heat,
Heart goes thumping, ups its beat.

The way you turn to look at me,
Make sure I'm there, yes only me.
That searching glance down to the lips,
Muscles flex in sensuous grip.

A special word quite soft and low,
Blushing creeps up, cheeks aglow,
Glance up and down, electric grip,
You try to hide, feelings slip.

Unspoken words, lie in our minds,
Unlocked, who knows what we would find,
Transmitted through a special look
Our eyes are like an open book.

Nobody else can see or hear,
Those currents felt when we are near,
Body language between us felt,
One touch and surely we would melt.

W Curran

A POEM TO MALCOLM

Brother, son, uncle, faithful friend,
Our missing you will never end.
You perked us up and calmed us down.
Always lovely to see you in Croydon Town.

So much reminds me of our bond,
Jaunts and walks and memories fond.
I've left the last Scrabble game we played,
You'd call through to the kitchen,
Where I'd have the tea made.

Remember those concerts,
The atmosphere in the stalls?
Queuing at the booking office
Of the Festival Halls.
Remember our outings and trips to the sea?
Will I again be in such good company?
After eating a sticky bun, I'd treat you
Like my little son and wipe your hands,
We did have fun.

I may get a hall carpet put down,
You called most colours, pink or brown!
You'd liked my red carpet,
Shall I have red?
Your departure leaves me with much unsaid.
A pity - we never made it, into bed?
Scrabble will never be the same,
Over 31 years, we played that game.

Innocents struggling to leave a mark.
Merry on photos, as if life were a lark.
With forces within, self-destruction and dark,
We concealed much stress, no picnic in the park.

Never did you go all out, to give pain,
Like 2 past Dodos, egotistical and vain.
Hey Malcolm! - I've just heard from Larraine!

Like those other comedians, Hancock and James,
Sherwood and Brenner are two indestructible names?
You should have been the one to go last!
What with you and this op, I've been a flag at half mast.

You finally got your tribute, toodlepip,
Off to the hairdressers, the surviving soldier must trip.

To remember our friendship from 1969 - 2000.

Carol Sherwood

THE MEANING OF LOVE

We love, our father
Also love, our mother,
The same, as we love,
Every sister, and brother.

We love, our new baby,
Whether it's a girl, or boy
And the love, they give back,
Gives us, great joy.

All children love sunshine
And most farmers, love rain,
Also we all love, good food,
Be it fancy, or plain.

So the meaning of love,
Is a four lettered word,
That is usually straight forward
Or sometimes, absurd.

Jean Hendrie

DREAMER

A dream of you in love's soft light
Your eyes reflecting my delight
With tears of joy that blur my sight
Diamonds in the moonlit night.

A dream of lips and whispered cries
That call my name in soft surprise
As we are one and passions rise
We reach the peak and share the prize.

A drift to you in dreamers land
And close to you I make my stand
To feel your caressing hand
Transport me to a wonder land.

A dream I kiss your lovely face
Your bright and then as pulses race
Drifting down through time and space
I kiss that other kissing place.

A dream as dreamer often dare
Of and loving souls laid bare
Locked in a topsy turvey snare
To kiss away each other's care.

Each night I dream and as I start
That dreaming journey of my heart
Across those miles keeping us apart
To give you love and love's sweet dart.

E A Parkin

LOVE AT FIRST SIGHT

My life was incomplete until you came
That early spring when winter's hold could still
Be seen on leafless tree and barren hill,
Denying warmer days their rightful claim.

You were so casual and did not seem
To be the kind of man I wished to know,
But forces strange and wondrous made love grow
And realised the substance of my dream.

Yet I was doubtful, thought it too intense.
Love at first sight was just stuff for fools.
It had no place in logic, made no sense -
A game of chance without a set of rules.
But I succumbed, and in my innocence
Was unaware that passion often cools.

Celia G Thomas

DIFFERENT LOVES

Love is something we experience at one time or another,
Whether it be for parents, sister, friend or brother,
An all consuming feeling of wanting to share,
The best things in life with those for whom we care.

Love often means sacrifice to give of the best,
Hard sometimes to achieve, when put to the test,
It has to be strong to overcome all life's temptations,
To bring out the best in all our relations.

The love of one's life partner brings you close together,
Enabling you to face misfortune, and setbacks to weather,
To give solace and comfort to face each new day
When illness and death beset your way.

Family love has to be the strongest tie of all
How often down the years can you recall,
When love enfolded you in its firm embrace,
As unexpected disasters were taking place.

And so we ask God His love to give,
To one and all, for as long as we live
And we in turn can be happy, and to others show,
That love which is fostered, will grow and grow.
If only into life the thread of love we weave,
How much happiness we'll give to others and receive.

E K Jones

THE HOUSE OF BLISS

Twas in my house we first met
and soon, our lips were poised for kissing:
Her eyes were filled with tears of joy -
her heart had found what was missing.

We stood in silence for many minutes
enwrapped in each other's arms,
Our eyes telling each other of our love,
and our hearts beating wildly, losing their calm.

From that moment on we plighted our troth,
the love for each other would never dissolve:
We clasped each other waistwise, firmly, and as
we kissed, promised always, to keep our resolve.

Our lives are now so full of happy bliss,
we have blue skies and sunshine every day:
Though there are times a few raindrops fall,
like the tides, they come, then go away.

So, from that day in my House of Bliss,
when our lips did taste our first enchanting kiss.
We're always so happy, and always so gay,
We do not want our lives, any other way.

Geo K Phillips

THE LETTER

I'm waiting for a letter but sadly it never came
Why is it when you are in love you suffer so much pain
I lay in my bed at night
Thinking of Mr Right

Then I start feeling sorry for myself
And start thinking of my plight
I remember when we took long walks
And he held me in his arms
And he smothered me with kisses
And found him so full of charm.

When he left me feeling blue
He didn't realise he was leaving two
Our baby was born at Christmas time.
It's right what they say that love is blind.

I remember all the loving care
And all the love we used to share
All that now is in the past and that letter it never came
So I'm just a lonely, frustrated woman suffering everlasting pain.

Bert Booley

WHAT IS WONDER?

What is wonder but to lash
Against the tide of desire and crash
Within the waves of a beating heart
To stop, to breathe and again to start.

I wonder at your eyes, deep, bright
And the melting into you at night,
At the laughting morning before we part
To stop, to breathe and again to start.

What is wonder but to adore
The pangs of love yet love the more,
To open our eyes although they smart
To stop, to breathe and again to start.

Robin Kiel

TRUE LOVE

Love will never fail,
Is what the scriptures say;
And true love will prevail,
The years that slip away.

Tom Ritchie

SUMMER OF LOVE

That first romance radiates far
Eyes a-sparkle - twinkling star.
Beauty blossoms abundantly
Such joy, laughter - just so much glee.
See great happiness everywhere
Summer of love for to share.
Those precious moments to hold dear
Memories bring much warmth and cheer.

Love so special and has no end
Everyone's forever friend.
May this light brightly shine alway
Then safely keep us night and day
A little tenderness to try
Wonderful times, spirits so high
Future dreams, sunny and bright,
Summer of love with such delight.

Margaret Jackson

SWEET CHILD OF MINE

Oh sweet, gentle child of mine
Take each step one day at a time
It doesn't matter what others say
I'll hold your hand all the way

One day you'll be free to skip and run
You'll feel the warmth of the summer sun
To play like other children all day long
And listen to the birds sing their song

For now see with my eyes, hear with my ears
I'll be here no matter how many years
One day you'll open your eyes and see for yourself
You're so beautiful, and a picture of health

Until that day sweet child of mine
I'll keep looking, hoping to see a sign
In my arms I hold you safe at night
Praying you regain your hearing and sight

Susan Rae Nott

HAVE YOU LOVED?

Have you ever loved someone so much that you can't look them
in the eye?
Can you tell his smell anywhere?
Recognise his voice? Do you blush when you hear his name?
Do you feel sick talking one word to him?
And get short of breath while thinking of him?

When this happens over one love,
Then and only then can you tell me that
I can't cry over him.
For when you feel all this - you're in love.
Tears of happiness or despair,
I have a right to cry as I'm in love.

Kate Stobart

LOVE'S FULFILMENT

All love to me seems wrapped in thought
Of dreams and visions made real.
Where life's unleashed strands of radiant light
Silently, entrancingly meet - and then reveal
(By outward sign of eyes)
Those depths, that soul
The tender calm of self-surrender,
The subtle half-sobbed sighs
Quaint expressions of love's serene repose
Choking tears - not of pain
Swept back - to rise again
Quietly subdued.
As with gentle firmness
The mind competes
Releasing softness, now imbued
With courageous responses, unashamed
Together we approach
Love's fulfilment
Described innumerably - yet still unnamed

Jack Graham

WEDDING BELLS AND FRAGRANT ROSES

Wedding bells and fragrant roses, will tell the fairy tale
Of a boy so charming and girl in flowing veil
Wedding bells and fragrant roses; bright smiles and tears of joy
As loving hearts beat gladly for happy girl and boy.

Wedding bells and fragrant roses in house of God so grand;
Where solemn vows are taken; and given, loves gold band,
Wedding bells and fragrant roses, a mother's gentle sigh,
As mem'ries of childhood, in mind go flashing by.

Wedding bells and fragrant roses, sweet bridesmaids starry eyed,
Page-boys dressed in velvet, angelic by their side.
Wedding bells and fragrant roses, hymn-sheets all snowy-white,
Awaiting young choir boys to sing their great delight.

Wedding bells and fragrant roses, sweet freesias in bouquet,
Horse shoes tied with ribbon, for good luck on display;
Wedding bells and fragrant roses, tradition shining through,
For bride, something borrowed, then old, brand new and blue.

Wedding bells and fragrant roses, on fruity cake so tall
Standing 'mid the splendour of decorated hall:
Wedding bells and fragrant roses, may they forever dance,
With dear wife and husband, to tune of 'Sweet Romance'.

Wedding bells and fragrant roses, best wishes warm and true,
Spanning sparkling oceans, and skies of powder-blue.
Wedding bells and fragrant roses, pray they each future year,
Say as romance blossoms, 'I love you still, my dear.'

Violet M Corlett

RETA: LOVE FROM ME TO YOU

My heart, my love goes out to you forever
Forever is the tomorrow of today
And my love for you my dear will never waver
As sure as night follows after day.

My dreams I have of you and I together
Exhausts me when I go on my way
And seem to bring along much duller weather
As being together is the light of every day.

I pray that God may never separate us
But unite us both together at His throne
That we may live in paradise forever
And enjoy the blessing of never being alone.

Bob

UNLESS WITH THEE

Don't look for me,
When I am gone.
'Neath churchyard stone;
Too sad the day.

But rather look,
Where children play;
Or out above the Milky Way.
Don't look for me
Where others lie;

But look for me,
Where larks do fly.
And otters splash,
And salmon leap;

And lovers who,
Rendezvous do keep.

If you would find
The likes of me
Let joy be in your memory.

I'm not in earth,
Where you left me.
I will not leave;
Unless with thee.

Windsor Hopkins

INDECISION

I sit by the phone
Should I give in, concede?
He did break my heart
Left it open to bleed.

He shattered my trust
Killed our love with one blow
Should I phone him and beg
Or just let him go?

Is he feeling the same?
Regretting his plan
I doubt it, unlikely
After all, he's a man.

With chin up I rethink
Contemplate life alone
Am I strong? Then again
Should I pick up the phone?

Lisa J Stuart

THE ROSE

Innocent and pure without a care,
Protected from man's alluring snare.
His chilling deeds like a winter's breeze,
Wishes for her heart to freeze.
A delightful surprise, an untimely birth,
Like a predator, he dances with great mirth.

Unhindered by nature, the petals fall ajar,
A lustrous red, the sweet scent travels far
Attracting the bee with his deadly sting,
She is unaware of this poisonous thing.
Still full of youth and willing to trust,
She gives into the growing feeling of lust.

His poison, like the sun, penetrates her life,
The unbearable pain, stabbing like a knife.
He is the sun, a burning fire,
Tempting her to give way to desire -
To give her love, her body, her soul,
To let him be master, to be in control.

Seasons fade away, the rose is still in bloom,
The obscured sky is filled with doom and gloom.
Her bright red cheeks seem to grow pale,
His love for her appears to grow stale.
Autumn has gone, his foliage is lost,
She sees his true heart, clouded over with frost.

Happiness is gone and her life begins to wilt.
Love has disappeared and the hurt is deeply felt.
The frost-bitten petals fall softly to the ground,
Like the rain, her tears, are falling all around.
With winter's new beginning and life at a close,
Her love has died forever just like the frozen rose.

Louise Turner

DAVID

I would like to put my feet up
My thoughts when leaving work
Thinking of excuses
For jobs I wished to shirk

The telephone was ringing
As my key was in the door
A friend was having a party
I felt oh what a chore!

Hastily I got ready
My feet will have to wait
As my friend arranged to meet me
At approximately half past eight

Arriving at the party
My heart just missed a beat
I gazed across the room
At the guy beside the seat

His brilliant blue eyes
Fixed me in a trance
And I really could not believe it
When he asked me for a dance

Loving at first sight
It really happened to me
I was so very happy
That everyone could see

If I had put my feet up
I would not have met my Dave
Now the husband I adore
And to whom my heart I gave

Lyn Collins

TRUE LOVE

True love
is like the warmth of summer's sun.
True love
is constant, does not wax or wane.
True love
shows compassion to those in pain.
True love
is never critical or harsh.
True love
consoles the broken heart.
True love
sometimes hides behind the mists of time only to reappear again.
True love
endures the complexities of life.
True love
is the greatest gift - you are my
True love.

Patricia Clarke

A Cold Moon

Stand with me,
hold my hand,
watch the moon
spread cold light
on a tired world.

If you are gone
by the next moon
the light will seem colder
on that same tired world
for I shall be alone.

Godfrey Dodds

LOVE'S SPARK

Love comes with affection,
And affection comes as love's friend,
The two, who together find the words,
To make broken hearts mend.

Shared - without the asking
In teenage years, by a girl and a boy,
Answers that need no question,
Of delights to be found, that two can enjoy.

Temptation - coaxes with enjoyment,
Opportunities to be explored,
Where 'no', becomes 'yes',
And 'yes', becomes 'more'.

Two young hearts,
- Whose tomorrow -
Owns more than yesterday,
Or today, ever will.

As love's flame bursts forth,
From what was only a spark,
- And like a log on a fire -
Together, they share a warmth
Which they never had before when they were apart.

Bakewell Burt

HURST GREEN

Heavenly peace seeping
Underpinning
Roots here and now
Seemingly settled
Therefore feeding

Green grasses well fed
River Ribble serving earth
Eden renewed
Eternal connected
Now.

Robert D Shooter

EACH OTHER

Giving to each other,
Is what it's all about,
Living for each other,
Without the need to doubt.

Hoping with each other,
That life will bring some fun,
Wishing for each other,
That dawn of radiant sun.

Owing to each other,
A debt of gratitude,
Loving one another,
When thoughts maybe, elude.

Pulling hard together,
When times require us to,
Making precious moments,
Stretch out for me and you.

John Cook

To My Mother, With Love

I have not felt the passing years,
But pass they have.
And in the time I grow much wiser,
That much you know too.
For together life is showing us
The well-worn path.
Long may we share the joy of loving;
As only mothers can.
Long may I see your youth
In my children, as you see yours in me.
The circles that ensure forever more,
A part of you is eternal.

Nicky Allis

THE GREATEST LOVE

I love him
Because he first loved me
With a love that binds
The heart.
With chains more soft than silk
And yet
More firm and adamant

I have life through his death
And peace through his blood
He was rich but for me
Became poor
I am able to say
With the saints of old
No ifs or buts, but sure.

Christine Williams

A TEAR FOR THEE
(Dedicated to Joyce)

My dearest dear,
    if only you could see.
This little tear
    upon my cheek for thee.
For would it say,
    how much I miss you so.
As day by day,
    my love for you does grow.
Then come the time,
    to your side I'll be.
I'll touch your cheek to mine,
    my tear be shared with thee.

John Clarke

LOVE STORY

I need to find love, a spirit above,
The cares of the day and its foam,
The daily routine, the world's sordid scene,
A place that is haven and home.

A soul that is free and full of sweet glee,
A mate that will strive hand in glove,
And out of God's press, true beauty express,
The sweetness and soul of a dove.

A true heart serene, at peace with her scene,
A lover of nature and art,
To erase what has been, as new vistas are seen,
Committed to make a fresh start.

Someone to undress, a lover's caress,
A woman both vibrant and pure,
That Cupid may bless to ease my distress,
A love that can grow and endure.

I sincerely believe that to give and receive
Is one of God's greatest gifts,
It raises our tone, to share, not alone,
Our spirit, then joyful, uplifts.

Though far I may roam a man needs a home,
An intimate nest built for two,
A safe, warm retreat where two hearts can meet,
And someone who cares, to greet you.

A duet for two that says 'I love you'
With feeling and meaning aglow,
To see the day through, a path that is true,
Together to blossom and grow.

A soulmate that's blessed and not just a guest,
Someone who will answer life's call,
Give meaning to life, a lover or wife,
The essence and salt of it all.

Emmanuel Petrakis

LOVE'S DESPAIR

I love her; my life has gone crazy and turned upside down.
Will I ever be sane again, when will I come around?
She belongs to another, I hope time is on my side,
Because I will wait forever, for chance to take that ride.
I wake in the middle of the night; she comes into my mind.
I can't get back to sleep again; my dream is so sublime.
She comes into my mind at work, in the middle of the day.
People ask why the silly grin; I'm not allowed to say?
Rumours abound, but nobody knows what is going on.
Things aren't getting out of hand; we're doing nothing wrong.
She probably wishes we had never met, perhaps gone another way,
But what is meant to be will be, just what more can I say.
With love you do not get a chance, too late to pick and choose.
Sometimes you get very lucky, but sometimes you most lose.

Ken Mills

JAMIE - A SPECIAL CHILD

Distraught at his birth
she cried a river of tears.
Loved ones couldn't console her.
A Down's Syndrome baby
placed in unwilling arms.
This child was not flesh of her flesh.
How could it be?
Nine months of waiting
dreaming and hoping.
This was the outcome, it was so unfair.

After the despair came the anger.
She raged and raged,
her heart was broken.
Why me was her silent scream.

Like an automaton she filled each day.
Lethargic, indifferent she no longer cared.
Then slowly the mists lifted,
she saw him more clearly.
He wasn't perfect but he was blameless
and needed her desperately.

Overwhelmed by emotion
she pressed her lips to his downy head.
'I'll take care of you my special child'
and her tears fell again
but gently this time.

Betty Paskin

IF I AM

If I am your wind, then let me be strong.
If I am your life, then let me be long.
If I am your trouble, then let me be fleet.
If I am your song, then let me be sweet.
If I am your beacon, then let me burn bright.
If I am your answer, then let me be right.
If I am your aim, then let me be sure.
If I am your love, then let me be pure.

K Leonard

LOVE ISN'T FREE

In today's world
love seems to be used sparingly,
just another word men use
to keep women happy,
to get what they want from them.

Maybe men need to check again,
women are taking control,
'I love you' is not enough anymore.
What can you promise me?
Wealth, security, honesty?

We won't just take a back seat,
we're going to be the drivers,
the ball is in our court now,
if you want love, you'll play our way.
We won't accommodate your cheating ways.

So if you say you love me,
you'll have to mean it.
Because my heart isn't free anymore,
it has to be earned, I've been hurt
too many times to care now.

Maybe one day I might love again,
but it won't be anytime soon.

Natalie Hooper

ROSARY

Rose Anne is a gentle nun
stepping idly in the sun.

Several rosebuds on a stem,
must she make an end of them?

Why must she her face avert?
Why contrary, why so curt?

Shall no thieving fingers dare
take a jewel from her hair?

Does she, smiling secretly,
hold a love-filled rosary?

Will she end as I've begun?
She is such a careful one.

George Pearson

LOVE OF A FATHER

Love comes in many guises
As we go on our way.
But one thread of love
Entwines our heart
Is always there to stay
It helped us in our childhood
On the eve of womanhood
Dried our tears and loved us
And always understood.
Rejoiced in all our triumphs
Soothed away our fears.
A father's love for daughter
Echoes down the years.
Close your eyes
He's with you still
He loved you then
And always will.

Gladys Mary Gayler

THE FOUR LETTER WORD

An excited breath-taking feeling that makes you bounce off the ceiling,
A smile on your face, that can't be replaced,
Something that's unseen, making your cheeks beam,
A bouncy feeling that makes you feel warm,
Something to shelter you from the storm,
Something that gives you energy and makes you want to run,
Laughter, laughter by the tonne.
Fire that comes and sets you alight, it cannot be touched
It's out of sight,
It comes down on us from a height above,
The four letter word, we call it love!

Leonnie Richardson

SHE IS GOLD

Her hair is like strings
Of gold as he runs his
Fingers through her hair.

He looks in her eyes
And sees golden amber
The colour of passion
And heat.

Her skin is like golden light,
Her face is the shape
Of a gold heart as he touches
Her lips they turn to gold
She smiles a golden smile
Forever.

Olive Irwin

THIS FAR

And must I love you child,
This far,
This far,
With love that cares for you
Where'er you are?
When you were small
I held you to my breast
And never knew
Someday I'd face this test,
To care so very much,
So greatly,
That I'd let you go.

Must I love you child of mine
This far,
This far,
And bear for you a smile
No trial can mar?
I loved you true
I gave you all I had.
But you were small
And days were somehow glad.
I could not visualise
A day
When I would let you go.

And yet I love you child
This far and more;
Right to the core;
And so I let you go,
Yea, even
Send away my dearest friend
With bravest smile until the end.
For ah,
I love you truly child of mine,
This far,
This far.

Christine Dennison

FUEL TO THE FIRE

You are the fuel to my fire
When you're so forgiving
You are the fuel to my fire
When you make life worth living
You are my dream
You are my heart
And maybe someday
Maybe some way
You'll be my destiny
You'll be my infinity
You'll be my wife
When we're together we shall live a happy life
When it's forever we shall overcome all strife
Our futures shall be just as nice
If not better
As always our love has no price
May these thoughts kindle in the mire
You are the fuel to my fire

You are the fuel to my fire
When you're so outrageous
You are the fuel to my fire
When desirably delicious
You have my lust screaming for you
You destroy all my blues
You're supreme
You're a dream
You're my queen
In the way that your body lures me
In the enchanting way you play me
With finesse
With dexterity

You are my master and my pawn
My jackal and my fawn
My lust is pumping blood
Drowning in your flood
You are so pure
That you allure
All my flame and desire
You are the fuel to my fire

Kevin Murphy

IF THERE WERE WORDS

If there were words to tell you
How much you mean to me
I'd gladly take a lifetime
Just to make you see

I'd swim my way through oceans
I'd crawl across the sand
I'd gladly do just anything
To make you understand

I love you with a passion
My heart's a raging sea
Every time I'm near you
The tides wash over me

There's no way I can help it
No reason I should try
My life would have no meaning
Without you by my side

Kelly Souten

QUIETNESS

Sitting quietly in my chair
I watch my grandchild deep in play
Absorbed within her world of dreams
Creating, acting out her childhood roles.
She concentrates upon the scene
Which only she can see.

Unconsciously she shakes her head
And tossing her dark hair she frowns
At some imagined deed
Of some imagined friend.

Her eyes meet mine
And light with love
Then flit away
To focus on her secret make-believe;
Her eyes are soft and beautiful
Seeing only innocence.

And she will never comprehend
The depths of love
I feel for her
Just watching her at play.

Ralph McMurray

WINE AND ROSES

Savour the moments
Taste the wine
Treasure these moments.
They may not last forever.
Roses may fade
But don't let love die.
Words said in haste
Don't let 'time waste'
So make haste.
Sort out your 'differences'
Time does not wait
Let happiness be now.
Roses may die
But don't let your love.
Have fragrant memories,
As time 'drifts' by.

Margaret Parnell

MY LOVES OVER THE YEARS

My dad, a gentle soul, a loveable softie
Mum the backbone, a tower of strength
Grandads and Grandmas, there for us
Aunts, uncles, cousins too
Sisters, we've stuck together
Friends seem to come over the years, or stay
My first love, puppy love, I'll never forget
Leslie, we walked down the aisle too young
Our love just fizzled out
My children, you're the best
My grandchildren growing up fast
Even I fell overhead in love
Oh the pain, he didn't feel the same
Not forgetting my film star crush
My Fred, my last true love
My rock, strength, comfort, a darling
He's in heaven now, keeping an eye on me
All these loves helped me,
Through my years of happiness
Also the tears I have shed.

Evelyn Farr

FEELINGS - TODAY

I've come to know you quite a lot, and I thought of you so well,
But what such revelations at the tales you had to tell!
At heart you are a tearaway, a rebel without a cause
I never thought I'd train you to live within my laws.
Then I was disillusioned . . . at lots of things you said
I really felt heartbroken, and a voice inside my head -
Told be to beware of you to get to know you more -
But I didn't think I wanted to - I was no longer sure;
Of the man I'd come to know, our views just weren't the same
You had your thoughts, I had mine - we didn't play the
                                        same ball game;
My life was very different, from the life that you had known
All I knew was hardship, and the good things just on loan.
Whereas, you had all the nice things, plus, you are quite fit,
You never have been homeless, our lives differ quite a bit;
I never think you understand - my life as it has been -
I never think you want to know - exactly what I mean.
We really are so different - our paths just do not meet -
And though we are compatible, you're just not up my street!
I'm nowhere ready to live my life, with someone I don't know
Or someone I feel inferior to, as in the end I'd have to go;
Couldn't fit in with the usual scene, the past has me well prepared -
For a future that's not very clear - that's why I'm runnin' scared!
Even if you had a crystal ball - or some tarot cards to see,
Or went to a fortune-teller, (and paid an enormous fee!)
I bet they couldn't tell you, of any future there for us
They'd say it all looked hazy, and something about a fuss;
Hardly a rosy picture, for anyone to see -
I think I knew, right from the start - we'd part, eventually.
But we had good times together - they really meant a lot -
But the past and present remind me - I'm happy with what I've got!

I Cone

MY WIFE, MY ANGEL

You left heaven to come to me
To give love and happiness to keep
Our time and days were full of joy
And your company I shall always treasure
When I meet you in my sleep

My sad thoughts that you have gone
Is a bitter life for me
But if God meant us to meet
And decided to take you first
It is his wish I must accept
And finish the work
I am meant to do on earth

I said you left heaven
And now back in God's care
Waiting for the day we meet
And another life to share

Dorothy Naylor

THE BACKS

Smoke rising
From the barricades
In 1949
The Morgan gang
Are baking spuds
The freedom flag
Is flying
Sun shining
On the waterfalls
Stickleback, pop belly
My heart is beating
Fit to bust
My legs have turned
To jelly

Rod Trott

A Many Splendoured Thing

Of course I'd heard, even talked about it!
So many kinds of love, but I felt relieved,
I was safe from all that, liked my 'Space',
Only for the young people I believed.

I knew I was happy in his company,
Admired his strength, felt secure,
I thought - this man could never hurt me,
Yes - but love? - Not for me that's for sure.

Love is *not* the prerogative of the young,
It was something I did not *need* to earn,
That's why I found, when it happened to me,
This was the lesson *I* had to learn.

Then our Saviour, knowing we were His,
Gave us a Beautiful Vision - ours to keep,
For love, if it is real, goes through dark days,
It's not all smiles - it can make you weep!

With Jesus, most important part of the equation,
We stood together, gazing in adoration at *Him*,
Receiving the golden glow of His Blessing,
- Shining on us - may it never grow dim.

Yes, Real Love comes in the person of Jesus,
He *is* love, only in Him will you see,
Because He died for us all - Love, Pure, True,
Eternal life - the best is yet to be.

Alice Carlin

IT MUST BE LOVE

What is this feeling within me,
I feel at the mere mention of your name,
The butterflies inside me start fluttering,
And I feel like a schoolgirl once again,
It's such a light-hearted feeling,
As if I'm walking on air,
Such a marvellous feeling,
That nothing else can compare,
When I know we are about to meet,
I'm trembling with anticipation,
Surely this must be love,
And not just infatuation,
My heart skips a beat,
As you come into view,
It happens with no one else,
Only when I look at you.

Anne Williams

GRANDPA

How could we let this day pass by
Without a tribute paid
The memories and laughter shared
The many games we played

From tiny tots through growing years
We loved your sense of fun
We knew how much you cared for us
For each and everyone

So many talents you possessed
Your great artistic flair
The way you loved creating things
Each detail planned with care

The influence you had on us
We never shall forget
Respect, affection mingled
Will stay with us as yet.

Enjoying life the way you did
You never did seem old
We really thought when you were made
They threw away the mould!

We loved your youthful energy
Enthusiasm, zest
Dear Grandpa, you have surely earned
Your long awaited rest

Sheila J Leheup

COUNTRY LOVERS

On a balmy summer's day
My lady friend and I would play
Then we would stroll down leafy lane
Listening to the drone of an aeroplane
Each other's virtues we would extol
Until we reached a grassy knoll
There we would lie amidst the hay
Whispering sweet nothings for something to say

There we would both sit and dream
Feeling contented and serene
A buttercup held under chin
To test your likes and dislikes - just a whim
When one gets amorous and vain
Clumsiness despoils a daisy chain
Then one's ardour is nullified and thwart
When a downpour of rain and it does abort

Francis Arthur Rawlinson

BORN TO LOVE

I was born to love you,
Fate wove her magic charms to fulfil
The desires, I find only in your arms.
Life offers no excuses for the way it
Deals each hand, all happens for reasons
We may never understand.
The words have yet to be created that
Could any way express how much you
Mean to me, you are 'my happiness'.
We have shared precious moments,
Your life has brushed with mine, and I
Will always love you,
Until the end of time . . .

Catherine Whyley

NULL AND VOID

Images disappearing; I turned, you vanished,
I grappled into the night, desperate to capture you,
Such an impromptu exodus severing all connections.
I felt denied, though this not your intention.

Which way to turn? All directions so foreboding.
My soul, an open wound solidified to protect,
Turmoil continued within, never ceasing.
What subterfuge I managed to create.

Days merging, self-destruction imminent.
Issues unresolved, many a lament for this.
No desire for the sorrow to be witnessed,
Begging that I be left until strong.

Dreams of a time when we laughed.
How near my thoughts ran.
A complete retreat into 'our own world'.
Yearning to revel in 'our memories'.
Frustration as I remained so far.

Will the present ever captivate me?
I long for you, no other can substitute.
You brought life into my marred world,
Your impact upon me immeasurable.
Treasured secrets continually remembered,
Can I weep anymore?

Chloe Gaudion

TO DIANA

I think of you each day my love
Though my mind be far away
My heart comes to the beech woods
Where we often used to stray
And your voice it whispers softly
In the wind among the leaves
And the world stands still a moment
As I listen to your pleas
That I should take life calmly
And not be ill at ease
Till that day soon when we'll both walk
Again among the trees.

Noel Craig Watson

WHEN LOVE GAMBLES

The waterfalls of fashion
Entangle life with lace
For a season of diamonds.

Smiles are whisked in corners
Of lipstick and toothpaste
Round the jail of boredom,

Looks drop from eyelashes
With the confidence
Of elasticated perfume.

Wrinkles alter the painful game
With lower stakes
And overlapping shame.

Marylène Walker

PAINTBRUSH

If my heart it was a paintbrush
They're on canvas, edged in golden love
A picture, painted in sighs, of a whispered hush

Stirred from wild emotions, from sights my eyes behold
Every stroke would be a memory
Carved from time untold

Susan E Roffey

COME MY LOVE

Come my love and lie with me.
Lay your sweet face next to mine.
For I would touch and hold you
tenderly and kiss those lips so
sweet and red as wine.

Come my love and let me whisper
those sweet words of love to you.
The secret thoughts and feelings
in my heart. Oh! Let me hear
those sweet words too.

Come my love and let me hold you
in my arms close, protecting you,
and see those eyes light and
sparkle as summer grass, lit with
morning dew.

Come my love for I need you so.
I am so lost and dead without you.
I need to feel your arms around me
and hear you say those words 'I do'.

You are here my love at last with
me, my heart is full with grateful
thoughts, of happy times that we have
spent together, happy in the love
that we both sought.

Now at last we live these precious
moments and you and I can be both
real and true, to ourselves in every
passing moment. Life's so sweet
when I am with you.

So come my love and lie with me.
Lay your sweet face next to mine.
For life though short is filled
with beauty and love, though brief,
can be as sweet as wine.

Terry Daley

DANIEL

Heart-shaped face and bright blue eyes
with a shock of light brown hair.
Hurts himself but never cries
just gives a look of devil may care.

His favourite video is Winnie The Pooh
and loves the antics he gets up to.
A belly laugh you will often hear
whilst a-watching from his chair.

He also loves to play in water
and does lots of things he didn't ought to.
Life is for living that must be true
especially when you're only two.

I hope one day a fine man we will see
'Daniel' my grandson,
I am sure it will be
as your sister before you
we all adore you.

Sheila Ryan

HEART LIFE

Not looking yet seeing
Not saying what we see.

The mind controlling our listening
Selective reporting.

Our minds clothe data
Warm thoughts light words
It is best to live in the heart
Only there may pain be put to flight.

John Rae Walker

OUR LOVE - A STONE

Some liken it to sun or moon or stars,
to bird song or the gentle summer rain.
Our love is stone.

Sometimes smooth, sea washed for centuries
or jagged, fresh hewn from a quarry face
but still a stone.

Oh, warm it is your hands my love, that I
may have remembered warmth when you are gone
and heart is stone.

Smooth and round like my breast in your dear hand.
Jagged and sharp like pain of love's desire,
that melts the stone.

Perfection plunged into the deepest pool
remains a thing of beauty, though unseen.
Thus is our stone.

Or is it one mined in the darkest earth,
its beauty all revealed by expert hands?
A precious stone.

At first a slab, sun-baked by suns of youth,
now worn and mellow as cathedral steps.
Oh! Such a stone.

A shelter from the storms and stress of life.
A refuge from the cruel world of time.
Our house of stone.

A stone was there where Adam's foot first trod
and will be there at Armageddon's call.
Our love, a stone.

Pat Izod

FRIENDSHIP

(This poem is dedicated to my friend Alf, in memory of all we stood for, in respect of one another and mostly of our friendship)

In was back in 1945 our friendship did begin,
Two twelve year old lads,
The pride of their dads,
With nothing to lose but to win!

We shared each other's hobbies,
We shared each other's joys,
We didn't stand on sorrow,
We were just two happy boys.

We developed an attachment,
From mutual esteem and respect,
From boyhood into manhood,
The bond has not broken yet.

So here's to my friend and our friendship,
Now fifty-two years have passed.
The pleasure's been mine, for this pal of mine,
Has given me memories that will last.

H Croston

MONOMANIA

You are the primrose in the lane assuring me of spring.
Those golden notes floating on air that make a blackbird sing.
All the freshness of a dawn still lightly kissed with dew.
An open road to Shangri-La. A window with a view.
Brighter than the sparkling stars when clouds and mists have gone.
Fairer than the glistening fire within an opal stone.
That lilting voice which calls me home when I am far away.
A gleaming candle in the dark holding the night at bay.
The culmination in my mind of a myriad of thoughts,
is reached as I look on the face that settles all my doubts.
Some may scorn my utterances but I without a qualm,
shrug and offer up a smile telling how crazed I am.
Yet you with equal madness know the virtue of its touch.
And versify in words, saying you want for me as much
as I so yearn for you. Such blessed insanity.
Who minds should we epitomise eccentricity.

James Feakes

WE HAVE EACH OTHER - DON'T WE

We have each other
Don't we
We have and at once share
In all things
Our minds and hearts
Where we might find each other
Warm and comforting
As in our life
Our conversation
But then this can be cheap
Although wanted it seems
As in one moment
We would have each other
As I thought then
Or what it is now
Yet this is worth something
If now given to someone else
Which might be expected
We had something
Really we had it all and it was all we could have
Everything as they are and fundamental
There can be something in a relationship
Wanted by all
Which if remembered might not be diminished
Either by time or circumstance present and past as are all our lives in
                                            important and wanted things
As the Earth turns and there may be new greetings.

C J Bayless

To My Wife

The years, they move at faster speed
The more and more that pass
They spin around, a gyroscope,
Accelerating fast

A feature of the speeding years
Is the joy that Christmas brings
And how it comes so fast around
To fly on Christmas wings

As a gyroscope is spinning
It holds its centre true
And a constant in the speeding years
Is the love I have for you

It isn't only Christmas
That we stop to speak of love
In retirement, all the days we have
We are as hand to glove

So growing old together,
We'll keep each other young
Thankful for the happiness
That our true love begun

Ray Ryan

WILLOW

No mouse is safe in the garden
She drinks from the pond with the fish
She wipes her nose on my trousers
Tuna is her favourite dish

I've seen her standing on the dining table
Sniffing at my flowers
She struggles to get her tummy through the cat flap
As she comes in from the autumn showers

She miaows for food again - she is greedy
She rubs herself against the chairs and settee
As she passes on her way to her food bowl
Making my suite as hairy as can be

She claws at the carpet and rugs
She never does as she's told
She lazes by the radiator
She doesn't like the cold

Her name is Willow and she's our cat
She's as spoilt as could be
And we love our cheeky, furry friend
But, she loves us too you see

Lyn Richard

THE PETALS OF LOVE

A rose with petals as soft as the breeze,
Falling so gently on the ground below.
Her straight green stem, bending in the wind,
As it disappears in the falling snow.

When in the summer, she stands tall and straight,
So proud of her gown of different hues.
In the warmth of the sun, she bursts into flower.
A rainbow of colours, pinks, reds and blues.

Then came the autumn, with wind and hail,
Pulling and tearing the leaves of her stem.
I watched her wilt and heard her cry,
As she slowly died in the falling rain.

I brought her inside, a few petals left,
And wrapped her in silk, like a shroud.
In a box trimmed with gold, I laid her to rest,
My petals of love, once so proud.

Just like old memories, once in full bloom,
Fade in the flames of a dying fire.
Or the haunting perfume of a certain room,
And the dreams she once did inspire.

Marion M Mason

THE COMING OF LOVE

The tide brought in a love for me
Across the land, across the sea
And then it ebbed and went away
For that love wasn't here to stay

The wind blew in a love for me
It was there for all to see
As the wind dropped and died away
So that love went on its way

The sun shone down your love to me
Filling me with ecstasy
Shining bright it made me glow
With the best love I'll ever know
For this love is here to stay
And will never, never go away

Diana Daley

An Old Memory Of Love . . .

Someone embraced me once:
A long time ago now . . .
Standing amidst
A forest of trees,
Turned by the seasons,
To gold, orange,
Yellow and red.

I remember the warmth
Of his body
Cutting through the
Sharp autumn air . . .
I remember
The smell of him . . .
Sweet and spicy . . .
Warm and comforting.

The memory
Is starting
To fade
Now.
The picture
Is dying
Away . . .
And as the memories
Of short-lived happiness
Die . . .
So do I.

Kirsty-Anne Wilkes

JUST US TWO AND ALBERT BALL

Left alone to read your letter.
'I love you, do not forget me.
You are in my heart if not in my bed.
Wish we were having a drink and a meal
At The Ely . . . '

You and I like going to The Ely.
Especially in the afternoon -
We've got the place to ourselves.

We often sit in the same corner,
At a table for four -
There's more room for the two of us.

We sit facing each other. We talk -
We are not pressed for time. We talk -
There's that special feeling between us.

It's all love . . . love and tenderness.
We raise our glasses of wine
(You prefer red, I prefer white),

We drink to the moment, to life -
You and I enjoy . . . life. Close to us,
Hanging on the wall, there is a photograph . . .

Of World War One fighter pilot
Captain Albert Ball - VC
He did not survive his 20th birthday.

Left alone to read your letter.
'I love you, do not forget me.
You are in my heart if not in my bed.
Wish we were having a drink and a meal
At The Ely . . . '

Claire-Lyse Sylvester

GEMMA

(My granddaughter)

You looked, I looked, we looked.
But your look searched my soul.
As your eyes scanned the very chambers of my heart,
My 'vision' was now clarified
With the remembrance of my 'lost youth'
Reflected in your innocent eyes.
It was a 'mirror' of my life gone by
'Is this the 'message' of a granddaughter's gaze?'
Is this the 'emotion' born to amaze,
How can I know what makes me see,
The 'love' exchanged from you to me.
You make my eyes look beyond just 'vision'
You are 'nature's child' just risen.
This blooming love shall not fade,
Because you are 'creation' and not just made,
This love we share, will take us far,
In all the 'heavens' you are my 'star'.
Among 'galaxies' of magic light,
You are my 'love' you are my 'sight' . . .

Bampi

GRANDCHILD

Give me a hug
A cuddle, a squeeze
Grandchild of mine
Please, oh, please.

You're the highlight
Of my winter days
Your efforts in growing
Deserve such praise.

You've learnt your colours
Letters and numbers
You gain knowledge
Beyond wonders.

Your life's an open book
Full of pages unfilled
Don't leave the furrows
Of life untilled.

Ann Weavers

IT TAKES AT LEAST A YEAR

It takes at least a year
For the heartache to subside,
Still the longing wells within you
Like the ever-surging tide.

The sadness of the one you've lost
Will gnaw into your brain,
And the memory of a simple tiff
Will fill your heart with pain.

A birthday date that haunts you
Whene'er it comes around,
A melody, a special word
Brings teardrops to the sound.

Those Christmases, those good new years,
The gifts you treasure most,
That first caress, that first sweet kiss
Those letters through the post!

That special day when bonds were tied,
And rings of gold exchanged,
That special place where first you met
And a date that you arranged!

Those dreams you had, the future plans
Of what and where to go,
It seems like only yesterday
It was oh! So long ago!

It takes at least a year
For the heartache to subside,
Still the feeling swell within you
As the never-ending tide.

Derek J Morgan

130

SPRINGTIME OF LIFE

Children shine,
their vibrant essence
life of spring.
They bring light,
wisdom and love.

Children thrive
in ever-growing
time of spring
and give verve,
laughter and joy.

Children flourish
like brightly coloured
flowers of spring
to share hope,
courage and dreams.

Katrina Shepherd

BEN

Sweet Ben, it saddens me to see,
How frail at times, you seem to be.
You came to us so full of life,
And yet you've had your share of strife.
A stray you were, so thin and coy,
As time went on, full of joy.
Your past we'll never know about
But your folks would miss you,
Of that there is no doubt.
You're slowing up now and then,
But you are still our cuddly Ben.
Your nature is so good and giving,
And you make the most of living.
It's hard to accept you are old,
And to think what the future may hold.
We thought we would lose you some time ago,
You were so ill, and we love you so.
With care you were soon bright again,
And we watched you return as our usual friend.
You look beautiful with your coat of blue merle,
Eyes shining, and mind in a whirl.
There are times when you have such energy,
So much more than I have in me.
You run around and play, such fun,
Tail wagging as you run.
Face alert with expression alight,
You're a joy to watch,
Such a wonderful sight.
In your years you are older than me,
But it's hard to believe when you run so free.

Whatever the future
Whatever the past
Rest assured Ben
You'll be loved to the last.
Stay with us please, for as long as you can,
Because we love you dearly, our little man.

Rosemary Fernie

SEQUENCES, MY LOVE

The first.
He is not hurting me;
I am hurting myself.
(I permit this)

The second.
I hate him sometimes for
what he has done to me.
(I allowed this)

The third.
I love and hate him that
he forced me to confront.
(The prisoned self)

The fourth.
It was not him but me;
I accepted his spoken truth.
(To free myself)

The fifth.
Is of the heart.
I could not love him more.

L A Churchill

THE WINDMILL ON THE HILL

Come picnic with me.
Come picnic with me.
The place with the old windmill,
Come picnic, come and see.
A place of natural beauty,
We don't have to make love my love
Let's make peace with nature, live a peace love.
Beside the windmill, beside the old windmill.
Hovering bluebirds, look where the wind carries the rain
                                          across the beacon

Hovering on minus wind chill above the trees.
Ants can have whatever they need.
Trees have leaves, we have wine and cheese.
Love can be such sweet melodies upon a hill.

Barry Powell

GOODNIGHT MY LOVE

Goodnight my darling, goodnight my love,
Goodnight, head laid upon a pillow, shared,
Goodnight, cheeks laid upon a bosom, bared,
The night to sleep the sleep of lover's rest
To dream of joys and sorrow, tears and jest -
The mixture that is one happiness today
But tomorrow, that more permanent to stay,
Your touch, your kiss, to you returned,
Wears out the night and hell is spurned,
I would prepare my being and my mind
Thus able, seeing, giving you in kind,
Goodnight my darling, goodnight my love.

Mervyn T Charleston

DEAR GOD...

If God is listening I want Him to know
That each and every where I go
I think of my father who passed away
I remember those things he would do and say.

If God is listening I want Him to understand
That in this world there is no other man
Who was as loving as my father and so special too
A father who cared for his children and guided them through.

If God is listening I want to make a plea
I want you to give my father the chance to see
His children grow up to fulfil all his dreams
Even though life is a struggle . . . well so it seems.

If God is listening high up above
I ask you never to deprive us of our father's love
If God is listening please let my father know
That he will always be remembered wherever we go . . .

Farah Gilani

GARDEN OF LOVE

I sit here in my garden and think of my lost love
And when I look at the flowers they remind me of her
When I look at the golden honeysuckle I think of the colour of her hair
When I look at the rosebuds I think of the dimples in her cheeks
When I look at the cream dianthus I think of her fair skin
When I look at the pink roses I think of her soft lips
When the young willow sways in the breeze I think of her slender body
When I look at the rose rambler twisted round the fern I think of how
Close we were and the love we had for one another
When I look at the fine grasses I think how frail she was
When I look at the moisture dripping from the leaves, I think of
The tears we shared on that last day.

Now as I sit here in my wheeled chair, pain creeping up my chest
I see a bright light at the bottom of the garden moving closer
                                   all the time
Now a shape has formed, then her gentle voice spoke, she said you
Waited and never married again all these forty years, she took
Hold of my hands and told me to stand up, I said 'My darling
I can't stand, neither can I walk,' but with her hands holding
Mine I found I could do both, she stood up on her tip toes
And kissed me on the lips, said 'How do you feel now?' I said
'I feel fine,' we turned and walked down the garden within
That bright light, she said 'Now we are together again let
Us both go home.'

Douglas Drummond

To My Love

I stood with you one happy sunlit day
Upon a tiny bridge o'er rippling stream
And told you of my love
'Neath sky supreme

A silver-winged seagull soared above
And trees made silhouettes against the blue
Where clouds were drifting by.

And then I knew -
As long as nature's wings caress the earth
And springtime's young green leaves are bathed in dew
As long as there is life
I'll cherish you.

B J Bevan

A UNION OF TWO HEARTS

I feel as one, in your life,
A union of two hearts,
A warming recognition,
Of all that love imparts.

This match was made in heaven,
So gentle and so pure,
For all life's pain and torment,
This love has been the cure.

The cure for past rejection,
The cure for tears we cried,
So now we smile, delighted,
Together, side by side.

Now, side by side we flourish,
And all our dreams unfold.
We soar just like a free bird,
Our future now foretold.

Our souls have been united,
We act and feel as one.
We swore to stay together,
Until our life is run.

We swore our true allegiance,
To each, we made a vow,
To join our hands in marriage,
And love has shown us how.

This love, we share together,
Is warm like summer rain.
A whole life, spent in searching,
'Twould never come again.

M J Plummer

THE GIFT OF TIME

Pleasure of knowing,
Two lovely, sweet girls,
Promotes joy, and pride,
More value than pearls.

Watching them grow,
From babes in arms,
Observing saucy antics,
Bath time of charms,
Knowledge of learning,
Progressed amid calm.
Patience presented
Few false alarms.

From nursery to day school,
Hands that held mine,
So small, and so soft,
Was comfort, sublime.
This gift to me,
Made my heart shine.

Lorna Tippett

SPIDER WEBS

Tightly woven threads of silver, all along the hedges spread
Gleaming, silver shawls of silver are the timid spiders' webs,
Hiding away from morning sunlight.

No inhabitants to be seen,
Silver splendour along the wayside,
Silver shawls o'er hedges green,
Through the morning mist they linger,
Till the sun comes shining through,
Then the silver shawls of silver
Disappears with the glistening dew,
Working hard and working willing
Every line patterned with care
Creating a diagram that is perfect
Spider's dainty hammock beds
If our lives had threads of silver,
Shining like the morning dew,
We would weave a Christian pattern,
God's grace and love a-shining through.

Spiders add their share of beauty, to our countryside,
When mist softly blankets the valleys.

Frances Gibson

The Babe

Clear-eyed in muted wonder was the gaze
That solemn-probed within the face of me,
Not knowingly to know or recognise
Some deep-laid mystery.

No hint of malice lurked beneath
The calm regard of those bright eyes,
No shrewd assessment prejudiced by doubt.
As silent pools behold the skies

In timeless wonderment of constant blue,
Of sorrow and corruption innocent,
They stared. And then they smiled.
I turned away content.

Elizabeth Hampden

LOVE IS A DREAM WE SHARE

There is a fire burning in my heart.
It was ignited by your love.
I feel so good I could soar so high
On the wings of a pure white dove.

There's a fire burning in my heart.
It was ignited by destiny.
I live for every passionate sigh,
And am glad you're here with me.

There's a fire burning in my heart.
It was ignited by true pleasure.
I feel so good I could sometimes cry,
And your heart I'll always treasure.

There's a fire burning in my heart.
It was ignited by a prayer.
I live for every tender moment,
Because true love is a dream we share.

Peter Steele

THE DEFINITIVE JOURNEY

I am warm, I am safe, laying here in darkness,
Surrounded in warm waters, I have been aware of being aware,
For some time now, hearing sounds, unfamiliar sounds,
That have become familiar, somewhere out there.
I rest a while, then I stretch, moving an elbow or knee jerkily.
As I grow the area is becoming less spacious.
Sometimes I try to turn around to find more room.
I feel somehow different, as if I am being pushed downwards,
The warm waters are rushing past me.
I am moving very slowly, but am being pressured to move on,
As I do, I suddenly feel restricted and am stopped,
A few moments later the obstacles free themselves,
I move on again, down and down, I am stopped again.
It is taking so long, where am I going?
An urgency inside me, tells me to go forward,
I move at speed now, the brightness is incredible.
I have left my safe haven, there is no water to breathe,
Something is holding me upside down, my rear has been slapped hard!
I gulp, I breathe, I am making a distressed sound.
The brightness is so strong, yet I cannot see, my eyelids remain closed.
I am being wrapped in something warm,
I am passed to something in a prone position, I hear inaudible words.
Suddenly I am being cradled by two loving arms.
A familiar sound is resounding, my head is being stroked gently.
The words 'Mother and baby girl' are exchanged excitedly.
I lay quietly wondering what 'Mother' is.
Then I recognise the voice holding me.
It was during those months when I was safe and warm,
The words would filter through as the outer wall of my chamber,
Was stroked tenderly, I understand now,
'Mother' was the one who protected me from the outside,
Of which I am now obviously a part.
But will 'Mother' protect me now? I feel it will all be fine,
But, what am I? And the noise and brightness is too much.

Amanda-Lea Manning

WHAT'S LOVE

At the school gate - when first we shyly met
You stole my heart and promised we'd never part
But come end of playtime - to different classes to go
But surely it would break - is all I know
It'll never last - but bring him for tea
Oh it will last - I think - they'll have to wait and see
When Christmas came - we wrote our notes
Together on paper of blue - up the chimney they flew
He wants a football - I want a skipping rope
Now it's up to Santa - our fingers crossed with hope
The school holidays - never seem to end
When you feel lost without your new friend
But is love like last year's building bricks
When you are only five and a half - and he is six

David Charles

REFLECTIONS
For Colin (Litttle H)

Eyes that sparkle, eyes that laugh and tease,
Stormy eyes that change as swiftly as a summer breeze.
Warm brown eyes under sweet dark brows,
They hold all the beauty nature allows.
Your eyes were made to give and please,
Then turn as cold as a winter freeze.
Hard and forbidding as a distant moorland tor
Brown as the bracken upon the windswept floor.
Beautiful as a moorland stream
I knew these eyes, but now it seems
They were just an illusion, a fantasy,
From some erotic dream.

Christine Yeoman

THESE HEARTFELT WORDS
(To someone loved)

Sleep on, sweet angel, through this quiet hour
Your softest breath is soothing to my heart,
You are to me the fragrance of a flower,
A masterpiece, a living work of art:
You are the toy which brings a child delight,
The warmest ray of sunlight shone at dawn;
The one which shrinks all shadows of the night
And sprinkles its resplendence on the lawn:
Though I'm awake and listening to the birds
Rehearsing songs of thankfulness and praise,
I'm moved to stave off sleep to think of words
Which suit and match the beauty of your ways.

And they are these, just simple words above,
Inspired by warmth, and written down with love.

Nicholas Winn

RHYME AND REASON

The captivating scent of a flower after an April shower,
The birds in chorus all day long,
The eerie sound of a tree swaying in a strong breeze,
The tempting smell of ripe plums in an orchard near Mum's,
The babbling stream where we paddled and dreamed,
The smoky aroma of burning logs, and the barking of the
                                        farmer's dogs.
The beautiful scene across the meadow so green,
With your hand in mine we forgot the time.
All these I add to the good times we shared,
Happy days when we were young and paired,
Now you've gone and I need to adjust,
I don't want to change but it seems I must,
I turn so many corners and you're not there,
The silence of the house I can no longer bear,
Until now I held on far too tight,
Afraid, lest you left my dreams at night.
Then I found the painting covered in dust,
The country scene with a pond, swans and ducks.
New life flowed into my empty hand again,
As I moved the brush on the canvas plain,
Now my life moves on with rhyme and reason,
There's new life for everyone in the right season.

Kathleen McBurney

Soul Thought

Going through my day.
Thoughts of him
with me all the way.
Looking round a crowded place
for staring eyes,
smiling face.

Bernadette O'Reilly